Archetypes

By Melanie Anne Phillips

Published by Storymind Press

Archetypes

By Melanie Anne Phillips
Creator StoryWeaver Co-creator Dramatica

Dramatica theory originally developed by
Melanie Anne Phillips & Chris Huntley

Introduction

Archetypes are not inventions, but representations of elemental human qualities. In fact each embodies a family of qualities not unlike families of elements in the periodic table. It is as if we put all the Rare Earth elements into one character and all the Noble Gasses into another.

This means that while each archetype has many component pieces, they all work in harmony to create a character of singular identity that we recognize as a facet of ourselves, made tangible, so that we might understand that aspect of our inner narrative.

Historically, students of story have identified a multitude of characters they have labeled as archetypes. As useful as these are for creating characters based on personality types, relationships, or subject matter, true archetypes have no role, no position, no purpose and no personality. They are the fundamental processes of our own hearts and minds made manifest, incarnate as functions within a narrative just as they are functions within us.

As an example, there is a *Reason* archetype to illustrate how our intellect approaches the problem at the core of a story. And in opposition, there is an *Emotion* archetype to exemplify how our passion comes to bear on the issue at hand. In totality, there are eight archetypes, each composed of eight individual elements, working in concert to illustrate the broad stroke primary colors of our psyches.

This book is a collection of essays that outline a cadre of archetypes, based on their underlying psychological foundations.

Origin of Archetypes

If archetypes represent basic human qualities, each assigned to a different character, then how would such a convention of story structure come to be? The answer lies in the manner in which people organize themselves in the real world, which fiction hopes to document and seeks to understand.

When we attempt to solve a problem as individuals, we bring all of our mental tools to bear on the issue. Each provides is a different take on the problem, calling a different kind of evaluation into play. In this way, we look for a solution from every angle we have and thereby understand the situation as fully as we are able.

When we gather in groups to solve a problem of common concern, we begin as a collection of individuals, each trying to explore the issue from all sides, as we do on our own. In short order, however, we begin to specialize, each focusing on a different approach to the problem that represents just one of our basic human qualities.

For example, one person will become the voice of *Reason* for the group, while another will become the group's *Skeptic*. In this way, the group as a whole is able to gain a deeper understanding of the issue because each specialist is able to devote full attention to just one aspect of the problem.

Thousands of generations of storytellers sought to discern the manner in which people interrelate and the roles they adopt. They observed the self-organization into the same specialties so often that the roles became codified in the conventions of story structure as the archetypes we know today.

And so, without anyone ever intentionally trying and without anyone ever realizing, the archetypal characters of fiction turn out to be perhaps the most accurate representation of the essential processes of problem solving we all possess, made manifest in an externalized representation of our own minds.

Players vs. Characters

Before we delve deeply into the nature and function of these representational archetypes, let us begin by stepping back a bit and asking a very simple but important question: What is a character?

This is not as easy to answer as it might at first appear. Like most dramatic concepts, it depends on whom you ask. Some say characters are just ordinary people in extraordinary situations. Others say characters represent personality types. And then there are those who see all characters as personifying ideals.

As varied as these descriptions are, they all share one thing in common: They are looking at characters through the veil of storytelling – the setting, manner of expression or topic. When we strip that away, we begin to see the true structural nature of characters underneath it all: past their personalities and into their underlying psychologies.

Still, before we delve into this fundamental *structure* of characters, let us give the devil his due and take a moment consider their personalities, as that is what makes them intriguing, involving, charismatic and memorable.

In a story, anything can have a personality: a person, an animal, a tree, the sea, a star, even a virus. This stands to reason because in our every day lives we imbue inanimate objects with human qualities when we name our boats, call the wind Mariah, or refer to the Fatherland, Mother Russia, or Lady Liberty. As a preliminary definition, we can call any entity that exhibits a personality a *player*.

Some players are just part of the background as with extras in the movies. Others are tools of convenience an author uses to drop information or solve a logistic conundrum in the plot. And still others are nothing more than window dressing – simple elements of entertainment that are purely storytelling devices.

But a player can also perform another dramatic task: it can function as part of the story argument. That is to say, it contributes to the problem solving process to illustrate which approaches work best in this particular situation.

When it directly advances the story's argument, the player has become a character. To be a character, then, the player must (through its attitudes and/or actions) illustrate one of the ways the story's central problem might be solved. And so, by this definition, not every personage populating a story is a character. Simply put: while all characters are players, not all players are characters.

To further clarify, consider this excerpt from another book of mine on the function of characters:

Characters need to perform double-duty in a story. First, they must depict fully developed people in the storytelling so that the readers or audience might identify with them and thereby become personally involved in the entertainment and, perhaps, internalize the message.

Second, each character must idealize a different facet of our own conflicting motivations, made tangible, incarnate, so that we (the readers or audience) might directly observe the mechanisms of our own minds, see them from the outside looking in, and thereby gain a better understanding of how to solve similar problems in our lives.

And so we see two distinct kinds of functions in each player when it also acts as a character: the fully developed aspect that makes it

10

a real person and the small fragment of our own psychology that makes it part of the story's argument.

Ultimately, as the story unfolds, all of these fragments will come together through the interactions of the characters like pieces of a puzzle to create the overall message of the story.

Armed with this understanding of the difference between players and characters and the two essential jobs of each character, let's focus on just the structural functional side where archetypes reside.

The 8 Archetypal Characters

There are 8 essential archetypal characters, each of which represents a different aspect of our own minds.

The Protagonist portrays our initiative, Antagonist our reticence to change. Reason is our intellect, Emotion our passion. Skeptic is our self-doubt, Sidekick our self-confidence. Finally, Guardian represents our conscience and the Contagonist is temptation.

Naturally, each must be developed as a complete person as well as in its dramatic function so that the reader or audience might identify with them. Yet underneath their humanity, each archetype illustrates how a different specific aspect of ourselves fares when trying to solve the problem at the heart of the story.

In this manner, stories not only involve us superficially, but provide an underlying message about how we might go about solving similar human problems in our own lives.

Here are the eight archetypal characters, described in terms of their dramatic functions:

PROTAGONIST: The traditional Protagonist is the driver of the story: the one who forces the action. Once it has accepted the charge to achieve the goal, it is relentless, even if occasionally beaten back.

ANTAGONIST: The Antagonist is the character directly opposed to the Protagonist. It represents the impediment that must be overcome for the Protagonist to succeed.

REASON: This character makes its decisions and takes action on the basis of logic, never letting feelings get in the way of a rational course.

EMOTION: The Emotion character responds with its feelings without thinking, whether it is angry or kind, with disregard for practicality.

SKEPTIC: Skeptic doubts everything — courses of action, sincerity, truth — whatever.

SIDEKICK: The Sidekick is unfailing in its loyalty and support. The Sidekick is often aligned with the Protagonist though may also be attached to the Antagonist.

GUARDIAN: The Guardian is a teacher or helper who aids the Protagonist in its quest and offers a moral standard.

CONTAGONIST: The Contagonist hinders and deludes the Protagonist, tempting it to take the wrong course or approach.

Protagonist and Antagonist Archetypes

Protagonist drives the plot forward.

Antagonist tries to stop him.

The Protagonist is the Prime Mover of the effort to achieve the Story's Goal. The Antagonist is the Chief impediment to that effort. In a sense, Protagonist is the irresistible force and Antagonist is the immovable object.

In our own minds, we survey our environment and consider whether or not we could improve things by taking action to change them. The struggle between the Protagonist and Antagonist represents this inner argument: is it better to leave things the way they are or to try and rearrange them?

The Protagonist represents our Initiative, the motivation to change the status quo. The Antagonist embodies our Reticence to change the status quo. These are perhaps our two most obvious human traits – the drive to alter our environment and the drive to keep things the way they are. That is likely why the Archetypes that represent them are usually the two most visible in a story.

Functionally, the character you choose as your Protagonist will exhibit unswerving drive. No matter what the obstacles, no matter what the price, the Protagonist will charge forward and try to convince everyone else to follow.

Without a Protagonist, your story would have no directed drive. It would meander through a series of events without any sense of compelling inevitability. When the climax arrives, it would likely be weak, not seen as the culmination and moment of truth so much as simply the end.

This is not to say that the Protagonist won't be misled or even temporarily convinced to stop trying, but like a smoldering fire the Protagonist is a self-starter. Eventually, he or she will ignite again and once more resume the drive toward the goal.

In choosing which of your characters to assign the role of Protagonist, do not feel obligated to choose one whose Storytelling qualities make it the most forceful. The Protagonist does not have to be the most powerful personality. Rather, it will simply be the character who keeps pressing forward, even if in a gentle manner until all the obstacles to success are either overcome or slowly eroded.

When creating your own stories, sometimes you will know what your goal is right off the bat. In such cases, the choice of Protagonist is usually an easy one. You simply pick the character whose storytelling interests and nature is best suited to the objective.

Other times, you may begin with only a setting and your characters, having no idea what the goal will turn out to be. By trying out the role of Protagonist on each of our characters, you can determine what kind of a goal the nature of that character might suggest.

By working out an appropriate goal for each character as if it were the Protagonist, you'll have a choice of goals. Developing the plot of your story then becomes a matter of choosing among options rather than an exercise in the brute force of creating something from nothing.

What, now, of the Antagonist? First, let us dispel a misconception. The Antagonist is not necessarily the villain. A villain, by definition, is essentially bad, immoral, mean or ill intentioned. These are all personality traits. But the antagonist is defined by its relationship to the goal, not by its intent or manner.

We have all heard the idioms, *Let sleeping dogs lie, Leave well enough alone*, and *If it works – don't fix it*. All of these express that very same human quality embodied by the Antagonist: Reticence.

To be clear, Reticence does not mean that the Antagonist is afraid of change. While that may be true, it may instead be that the Antagonist is simply comfortable with the way things are or may

14

even be ecstatic about them. Or, he or she may not care about the way things are but hate the way they would become if the goal were achieved.

Functionally, the character you choose as your Antagonist will try anything and everything to prevent the goal from being achieved. No matter what the cost, any price would not seem as bad to this character as the conditions he or she would endure if the goal comes to be. The Antagonist will never cease in its efforts, and will marshal every resource (human and material) to see that the Protagonist fails in his efforts.

Without an Antagonist, your story would have no concerted force directed against the Protagonist. Obstacles would seem arbitrary and inconsequential. When the climax arrives, it would likely seem insignificant, full of sound and fury, signifying nothing.

In choosing one of your characters as the Antagonist, don't be trapped into only selecting a mean-spirited one. it may well be that the Protagonist is the Bad Guy trying to do something terrible and the Antagonist is the Good Guy try to stop it. Or, both may be Good or both Bad.

The important thing is that the Antagonist must be in a position in the plot to place obstacles in the path of the Protagonist. Since the drive of the Protagonist is measured by the size of the obstacles he or she must overcome, it is usually a good idea to pick the character who can bring to bear the greatest obstacles.

Ask yourself which of your characters would have the most to lose or be the most distressed if the goal is achieved. That will likely be your Antagonist. But don't discount the other candidates out of hand. In storytelling, characters are not always what they seem. Even the character who seems most aligned with the Protagonist's purpose may have a hidden agenda that makes them the perfect choice for Antagonist. You might play such a character as an apparent aid to the effort, and later reveal how that character was actually behind all the troubles encountered.

Reason and Emotion Archetypes

The *Reason* Archetypal Character makes decisions and takes action wholly on the basis of logic. (Remember, we say *wholly* because we are describing an *Archetypal* Character.)

While the Reason archetype is the organized, step-by-step type the Emotion archetype is frenetic, disorganized, and driven by feelings.

It is important to note that, as in real life, Reason is not inherently better than Emotion, nor does Emotion have the edge on Reason. They just have different areas of strength and weakness that may make one more appropriate than the other in a given context.

Functionally, the *Emotion* Character has its heart on its sleeve; it is quick to anger, but also quick to empathize. Because it is frenetic and disorganized, however, most of its energy is uncontrolled and gets wasted by lashing out in so many directions that it ends up running in circles and getting nowhere.

In contrast, the *Reason* Character seems to lack "humanity" and has apparently no ability to think from the heart. As a result, the *Reason* Character often fails to find support for its well-laid plans and ends up wasting its effort because it has unknowingly violated the personal concerns of others.

In terms of narrative psychology, *Reason* and *Emotion* describe the conflict between our purely practical conclusions and considerations of our feelings. Throughout a story, the *Reason* and *Emotion* Archetypal Characters will conflict over the proper course of action and decision, illustrating the Story Mind's deliberation between intellect and passion.

Sidekick & Skeptic Archetypes

The *Sidekick* and the *Skeptic* represent the conflict between confidence and doubt in the Story Mind. The Sidekick is the faithful supporter. Usually, a Sidekick is attached to the Protagonist. Sometimes, however, they may be supporters of the Antagonist such as Renfield to Dracula.

This gives a good clue to the way we should look at functional characters: The purpose of the Sidekick is to show faithful support. That does not determine *who* or *what* it supports, but just that it must loyally support someone or something. Other dynamics of a story will determine who the Sidekick needs to be attached to in order to make the story's argument, but from the standpoint of just describing the Archetypal Characters by themselves, the Sidekick faithfully supports.

The Sidekick is balanced by the Skeptic. Where the Sidekick has *faith*, the Skeptic *disbelieves*; where the Sidekick *supports*, the Skeptic *opposes*. The nature of the Skeptic is nicely described in the line of a song… "Whatever it is, I'm against it." In the Story Mind, it is the function of the Skeptic to note the indicators that portend failure. In contrast, the Sidekick notes the indicators that point to success. The interactions between Sidekick and Skeptic describe the Story Mind's consideration of the likelihood of success.

Guardian & Contagonist Archetypes

What are the Guardian and Contagonist?

The first of these archetypes is a common yet often loosely defined set of functions; the second archetype is unique to the Dramatica theory of story structure. The Guardian functions as a teacher/helper who represents the Conscience of the Story Mind. This is a protective character who eliminates obstacles and illuminates the path ahead. In this way, the Guardian helps the Protagonist stay on the proper path to achieve success.

Balancing the Guardian is a character representing Temptation in the Story Mind. This character works to place obstacles in the path of the Protagonist, and to lure it away from success. Because this character works to hinder the progress of the Protagonist, we coined the name "Contagonist".

Contagonist: "Whose side are you on?"

Because the *Contagonist* and *Antagonist* both have a negative effect on the Protagonist, they can easily be confused with one another. They are, however, two completely different archetypes because they have two completely different functions in the Story Mind. Whereas the Antagonist works to stop the Protagonist, the Contagonist acts to deflect the Protagonist. The Antagonist wants to prevent the Protagonist from making further progress, the Contagonist wants to delay or divert the Protagonist for a time.

As with the Sidekick, the Contagonist can be allied with either the Antagonist or the Protagonist. Often, Contagonists are cast as the Antagonist's henchman or second-in-command. However, Contagonists are sometimes attached to the Protagonist where they function as a thorn in the side and bad influence. As a pair,

18

Guardian and Contagonist function in the Story Mind as Conscience and Temptation, providing both a light to illuminate the proper path and the enticement to step off it.

More About the Contagonist

The following excerpt is taken from an online class I hosted on the Dramatica Theory of Story. It is rather meandering, though full of interesting tidbits. If you feel it bogging you down, just skip it for now move on to the next article:

Dramatica Class Transcript – The Contagonist

William S1 : Could you touch on Contagonist?...

Dramatica : Sure, William! First of all, Dramatica sees 8 archetypal characters. But, Dramatica also sees Millions of non-archetypal characters. It all depends upon how the character elements are combined. The elements fall into "families", by their natures. Some are Motivations, some arc Methodologies, some are the character's Purposes. Others are their Means of Evaluation. There is an internal and external trait, in each of these four categories, and there are sixty-four elements all together.

That means that there is one special arrangement in which eight characters each get eight traits. And when all eight traits are from the same "family" it forms an archetypal character.

These characters are defined by the elements they contain. Guardian has Conscience, and Help among others. Contagonist has the dynamically opposed elements of Temptation, and Hinder. Reason has Control, and Logic. Emotion has Uncontrolled and feeling.

William S1 : What is the difference between the dramatic purpose of Antagonist and Contagonist?

Dramatica : As you indicate, the Contagonist is not the Antagonist. In terms of difference, the Antagonist is made up of

19

Avoid (or prevent) and Re-consider. This is dynamic to the Protagonist who is Pursue, and Consider. In other words, the Antagonist is out there to stop the Protagonist, but the Contagonist is just trying to push the Protagonist off the path, Look at conscience and temptation fighting it out. That is the job of Obi Wan and Darth [in the original *Star Wars*].

William S1 : Can the Contagonist be thought of as the Antagonist's ally?

Dramatica : Actually, William, it is only a storytelling convention that often the Contagonist is the Antagonist's ally. But they might also be attached to the Protagonist as well. You see, when we are looking at archetypal characters, we are not seeing them by their relationship to the Protagonist, but by their function in the story at large. The Contagonist Tempts and Hinders. They will do it to everyone everywhere, not only to the Protagonist.

The Story Behind the Contagonist Archetype

"Contagonist" is a name invented by Dramatica co-creator, Chris Huntley, to describe an archetype we hadn't seen identified in our writing classes at USC. Here's how the notion and the name came about:

When creating the Dramatica theory of story, we began with characters – archetypes to be specific. We jotted down all the familiar ones – Protagonist, Antagonist, Reason, Emotion, Sidekick, Skeptic and Guardian. But we had a problem...

First of all they all paired up except the Guardian: Protagonist/Antagonist, Reason/Emotion, Sidekick/Skeptic (faithful supporter / doubting opposer). But the Guardian (essentially a helper/protector who is also the voice of conscience) just hung out there alone.

We suspected that stories had symmetry (though we didn't know for sure at that time and none of our instructors had ever said anything about that). But, we really didn't know what this *missing* character should be, or what to call it.

When we were initially deriving our archetypes from the original Star Wars movie (episode IV – the original one) and saw that Protagonist/Antagonist were Luke/Darth (or so we initially thought). Reason/Emotion were Leia/Chewbacca, Sidekick/Skeptic were the Droids/Han Solo and the Guardian was Obi Wan.

But then, if Darth was the antagonist, what role did the empire under the command of the Gran Mof Tarkin play? After giving it much thought, we realized that while Darth comes off, especially in the opening scene, as the quintessential melodramatic villain, he is quickly relegated to the role of henchman for the Empire.

So, at first, we thought that the last archetype was Henchman. But after more thought, we realized that a Henchman was more like a Sidekick to a Villain. But after even more thought we determined that there was only one Sidekick, but he might be associated with either the Hero or the Villain. For example, Renfield (Dracula's assistant) is actually the Sidekick in that story (a faithful supporter) even though he works for the bad guy. And so, we concluded that a henchman was just a Sidekick in wolf's clothing.

But then we realized that Darth wasn't just a pain in the neck to our heroes, but he was also a thorn in the side of Tarkin and the Empire. Darth chokes one of the other commanders and he is the one who comes up with the plan to let the Millennium Falcon escape with a homing beacon, which leads to the demise of the Death Star ("I'm taking an awful chance, Vader," says Tarkin. "This had better work," indicating it is Darth's idea.)

So, if Darth screws up both sides, we realized he was similar to the archetype of the Trickster. But, he also represented the dark side of the force – the temptation of the dark side.

And then we had it. Darth was actually the opposite of Obi Wan. Rather than functioning as Obi Wan's *help* and *conscience*, Darth represented *hinder* and *temptation* – the exact opposites. So Obi Wan /Darth represented a pair of archetypes, completing the symmetry of that part of story structure.

But – what to call that character? He wasn't really a trickster, but more like a monkey wrench in the plans of both sides. And, he was also the tempter. So, Chris considered that this new archetype was against both the Protagonist and the Antagonist, and cleverly named him the Contagonist. Con (*against* in one language and *with* in another) Protagonist/Antagonist: Contagonist.

Since then (some 22 years ago as of this writing), I've seen the word creep into a number of literary discussions on the Internet that don't mention Dramatica at all. So, I suppose that's a good indicator it is becoming part of the overall language of story.

Now, if only my spell checker would recognize it!

"Hero" is a Stereotype NOT an Archetype!

In an article I published elsewhere on what sets *Objective Characters* apart from *Subjective Characters*, I described how Objective Characters represent dramatic functions in a story whereas Subjective Characters represent points of view.

The Protagonist is an example of an Objective Character whose function is to be the prime mover in the effort to achieve the story's goal. The Main Character is an example of a Subjective Character as it represents the *audience position* in a story – a point of view.

Authors frequently assign the roles of both Protagonist AND Main

22

Character to the same *player* in the story, creating the stereotypical "Hero". (Note that a Hero is a stereotype, not an archetype. The function of a Protagonist is archetypal, but combining that function into the same player as the one assigned as the audience position in the story – the Main Character – is a convention of storytelling, not a necessity of dramatic structure. This makes a Hero a stereotype, rather than an archetype.

The Protagonist Does Not Have To Be The Main Character

The following excerpt is taken from the Dramatica Class Transcripts:

Dramatica : The Main Character is not necessarily the Protagonist. First of all, a Protagonist is an archetypal character, and although archetypes work just fine, there are an infinite number of other kinds of more complex (and more simple) characters that can be created. But suppose we have a story with a Protagonist, and the Protagonist is NOT the Main Character... A story like *To Kill a Mockingbird*.

In *To Kill a Mockingbird*, Atticus, the Gregory Peck part in the movie, is the Protagonist. He is the driver of the Objective story – the story all the characters are concerned with. He is the one who wants to have the black man wrongly accused of rape freed.

The antagonist of the story is Bob Ewell, the father of the girl who was supposedly raped. He wants to have the man executed legally or at least lynched. But, the Main Character, the one through whose eyes we see the story through is Scout, Atticus' little girl. The audience identifies with her, and even the camera angles in the movie are from her eye level whenever she is in a scene.

In this story, the Obstacle Character is not the antagonist either. The Obstacle character is Boo Radley, the "boogie man" from next door. The author of the work, Harper Lee, in dealing with prejudice, did a very clever thing in separating the Main and Obstacle from the Protagonist and Antagonist. No one wants to admit they are prejudiced. So, in the Objective story, the audience looks AT Atticus and Bob Ewell, and passes judgment on them. But at the same time, we are sucked into being prejudiced ourselves from the very first scene, because of the way Scout feels about Boo.

At the end of the story, we realize emotionally, that we were just as wrong as the objective characters were. Very clever technique! About to change subject, any questions?

Dan Steele : Okay, clear on the functions/differences of Main/Protagonist/Obstacle Chars.

Dramatica : Great!

RDCvr : what is the difference between obstacle character and antagonist?

Dramatica : The Antagonist tries to prevent the Protagonist from achieving the story's goal, the Obstacle character tries to get the Main Character to change their belief system.

RDCvr : Okay.

Dramatica : They do this by building an *alternative paradigm* to the one the M.C. has traditionally used. More often than not, the M.C. and Protagonist characters are put in the same "body" and so are the Antagonist and Obstacle.

Dan Steele : Fine, but what if the antagonist is the protagonist, as in man against himself?

Dramatica : In Dramatica, we call any *body* that holds a character a *player*. Actually, you have touched on some very important theory points. First of all, when it comes to the Antagonist and Protagonist and all the other "objective" characters, the audience sees them "objectively" from the outside. Therefore, we identify them by their function in the story.

Again, we can feel for them, but we must see their function in order to understand the meaning of the battle. So, putting two objective functions that are diametrically opposed into the same player, mask the function of each, and make it VERY difficult to see what their purpose is. However, in stories like "Dr. Jeckyl and Mr. Hyde", or Sibyl, there are many objective characters in the same body, but not at the same time!

In fact, each is identified as a separate character, and each has its day in the sun. But the Main and Obstacle characters are not identified by function, but by point of view. The Main Character is "*I* "to the audience: first person singular. The Obstacle character is *you*. Second person singular. So, the Antagonist might be the Main Character, or the sidekick, or the Guardian or any objective character.

Dan Steele : Hmm. Am wondering though how this copes with internal psychological conflicts of a "tormented" Main character no, make that a Protagonist.

Dramatica : Well, the Main character, being a point of view is where all that internal conflict is seen.

RDCvr : But usually you also have external conflict which reflect or push the internal, no?

Dramatica : It is important to remember that when you combine a Protagonist in the same body as a Main character, the Protagonist part tries to drive the story forward to the goal, but the M.C. part is the INTERNAL conflict of the story, and can be full of angst.

Dan Steele : Okay.

Dramatica : They just don't HAVE to be in the same *body*. You need to separate the Objective or analytical part of the story's argument, from the Subjective or passionate part of the argument in order to map out all of each side. In a finished story, of course, they are all ultimately blended together through storytelling as part of the story's overall mind – its map of how to go about solving a particular kind of problem.

Archetypes and Character Elements

Excerpt from an upcoming book of mine on story structure:

In the Periodic Table in chemistry, elements are arranged in families in which all of its member elements share certain attributes. While they each have individual differences, a family resemblance between, say, Fluorine and Chlorine is as hard to miss as that in some human family lines.

In a like manner, the character elements can also be organized into families of similar traits called Archetypes. Each archetypal family contains exactly eight elements and, collectively, they form an entire facet of the Story Mind and, by extension, of our own minds.

The names of some of these archetypes are familiar: Protagonist and Antagonist, for example. But that creates a problem. The term archetype has been used by so many others, from Jung to Campbell, that it carries a great deal of baggage. The words Protagonist and Antagonist carry even more. So for Dramatica to come along and try to redefine those terms is to be fighting a lot of inertia and preconceptions.

Still, the traditional archetypes are looking at the same character functions as Dramatica, just through the obscurity of storytelling. So Dramatica is not so much redefining the archetypes as it is clarifying them. With that caveat in mind, let us proceed.

Each archetype exists to portray one of the major facets of our minds in a story. In a sense, each presents a different kind of argument, just as we work out a problem in our own thinking from several directions. Perhaps the two archetypes that most easily illustrate this point are Reason and Emotion.

The Reason archetype represents our intellect and the Emotion archetype, our passion. Certainly Reason and Emotion are two of the largest contributing factors in any decision we make in life. So it stands to reason (and feels about right) that they must be present in any story for its argument to be complete.

Turning now to the best known archetypes, Protagonist and Antagonist, we find that they are heavily masked by the storytelling concepts of Hero and Villain. While a Protagonist can be a Hero, that role is just one set of clothes it might wear. In fact, your Protagonist might as easily be a Villain. (And, in a like manner, an Antagonist might be Villain or Hero, for as we shall later see, both Hero and Villain are not archetypes but Stereotypes, which are over-used combinations of structural and storytelling elements working together.)

When you pare the Protagonist and Antagonist down to their structural bare bones, Protagonist represents our initiative and Antagonist, our reticence. In simpler terms, the Protagonist stands in for that part of ourselves that gets us up out of our chairs to get things done; to accomplish something. The Antagonist, in contrast, is the avatar of our desire to maintain the status quo, or more colloquially, to let sleeping dogs lie.

This fits in well with our common understanding of a Protagonist as the character leading the effort to achieve the goal and the Antagonist as the one who will do anything to stop him. (Note that while it stands for reticence, the Antagonist is not lazy or inactive, but rather exemplifies that counter-force within our own minds that acts in opposition to change: i.e. "If it works, don't fix it.")

We've just covered a lot of new ground, so let's pause for a moment to take stock: Groups of elements share certain family traits. When a whole family of elements is represented by a single character it is called an Archetype. Each archetype represents one of the major families of thought that go on in our own minds as we seek to resolve life's problems.

Archetypes & Complex Characters Together

A single story may have both Archetypal and Complex Characters. The decision of how to group the functions is completely open to an author's storytelling desires. The problem is, until one is aware of exactly what these functions are and how they relate, it is impossible to make meaningful decisions about how to combine them. These essential functions are at such a basic level that they form the elemental building blocks of Objective Characters. Therefore, we refer to these functions as character *Elements*. Listing them gives no feel for the end product, much as just listing the Periodic Chart of Elements in chemistry gives no feel for the natures of the compounds that might be engineered through combining them.

As a result, the best way to present the character Elements with meaning is to start with the Archetypal Characters (who by definition contain all the Elements) and break them down, step by step, level by level, until their elemental components are exposed. In this manner, understanding is carried down to the Elements, which may then be combined in non-archetypal ways to create Complex Characters.

Action & Decision Elements of Character Archetypes

Each of the Eight Archetypal Characters contains one characteristic pertaining to actions and another characteristic pertaining to decisions.

PROTAGONIST

Action Characteristic: Pursues the goal. The traditional Protagonist is the driver of the story: the one who forces the action.

Decision Characteristic: Urges the other characters to consider the necessity of achieving the goal.

ANTAGONIST

Action Characteristic: The Antagonist physically tries to prevent or avoid the successful achievement of the goal by the Protagonist.

Decision Characteristic: The Antagonist urges the other characters to reconsider the attempt to achieve the goal.

GUARDIAN

Action Characteristic: The Guardian is a helper who aids the efforts to achieve the story goal.

Decision Characteristic: It represents conscience in the mind, based upon the Author's view of morality.

CONTAGONIST

Action Characteristic: The Contagonist hinders the efforts to achieve the story goal.

Decision Characteristic: It represents temptation to take the wrong course or approach.

REASON

Action Characteristic: This character is very calm or controlled in its actions.

Decision Characteristic: It makes its decisions on the basis of logic, never letting emotion get in the way of a rational course.

EMOTION

Action Characteristic: The Emotional character is frenzied or uncontrolled in its actions.

Decision Characteristic: It responds with its feelings with disregard for practicality.

SIDEKICK

Action Characteristic: The Sidekick supports, playing a kind of cheering section.

Decision Characteristic: It is almost gullible in the extent of its faith — in the goal, in the Protagonist, in success, etc.

SKEPTIC

Action Characteristic: The Skeptic opposes — everything.

Decision Characteristic: It disbelieves everything, doubting courses of action, sincerity, truth — whatever.

Archetypal Characteristics in Quads

Having split them in two, we can see that each of the Archetypal

Characters has an attitude or Decision characteristic and an approach or Action characteristic. When we arrange both characteristics under each of the eight Archetypes in our Driver and Passenger Quad format, we get a graphic feel for the Archetypal Objective Characters and the Elements they represent.

Driver Quad

PROTAGONIST
Pursue-Consideration

GUARDIAN
Help-Conscience

CONTAGONIST
Hinder-Temptation

ANTAGONIST
Prevent-Re-consideration

Passenger Quad

SIDEKICK
Support-Faith

EMOTION
Uncontrolled-Feeling

REASON
Control-Logic

SKEPTIC
Oppose-Disbelief

In Dramatica, we refer to these 16 characteristics as the Motivation Elements because they describe what drives the Archetypal Characters.

Archetypes and the Crucial Element

A writer recently asked:

Is it necessary to have the main character as one of the archetypes?

No. The Main Character point of view must be attached to one of the character elements, not necessarily to an archetype. A story can have no archetypes if it uses nothing but complex characters, each representing one or more elements.

In a perfect structure, the Main Character (first-person point of view in the story) should be attached to the Crucial Element. The Crucial Element is the character attribute at the heart of the story's message. It is the lynchpin that describes both the underlying human quality that drives the Main Character and the element of the overall story that holds the key to achieving the goal.

Each character element represents a human quality or attribute. You can combine them in many ways, just as they are in real people. But one of those attributes will be the subject of the story at large – the human quality that is under examination by the author. That element must be possessed by the Main Character so that the readers/audience can stand in the shoes of that character and feel what it is like to possess the attribute in question. Naturally, the Main Character can also possess other elements, but the Crucial Element is a must.

There is one exception to this, and that is if the Crucial Element is possessed by the *Obstacle* Character (also called the *Influence* Character) rather than the Main Character. In this case, the Main Character will possess the "opposite" quality to that of the Crucial Element. (Whether the Crucial Element is with the Main or Obstacle Character determines where you are positioning the readers/audience in regard to the attribute under study – do you want them to feel as if they have the quality or are simply observing the quality – do you want them to be on the side of the argument or on the opposite side of the argument?

A second question:

Do you think it could work having the main character as the skeptic, whose sidekick provides the conflict as well as the support?

Actually, If you are using archetypes, the Main Character can be any archetype – even the Antagonist. As you surmised the Skeptic and Sidekick archetypes are opposites. The Sidekick is the faithful supporter and the Skeptic is the doubting opposer. So, if the Main Character were the Skeptic, the issue at the heart of the story's argument would be doubt or opposition. The Obstacle Character would then be the Sidekick and contain the opposite element (or the reverse, if the Crucial Element is given to the Obstacle).

One problem that occurs with pure archetypes – the Crucial Element Main/Obstacle relationship forces the Obstacle Character to be the opposite archetype to that of the Main Character. For example, if the Main Character is the Protagonist, then the Crucial Element function will require the Obstacle Character to be the Antagonist.

This causes difficulties because the plot struggle over the goal will be between Protagonist and Antagonist, and the same two people will duke it out over the Crucial Element as Main Character and Obstacle Character. This is hard to follow for a reader/audience since they have trouble separating the plot argument about the best way to go about achieving the goal from the personal argument about the best human quality to possess.

This often leads to melodrama, which occurs because (with both arguments intertwined) the author lets the excitement and energy of one of the arguments bridge the gap over holes in the other argument. In fact, both arguments often end up with holes

34

because the passionate moments of one of the arguments masks holes in the other. So, neither argument is full developed and it is only the strength of the storytelling that carries the story forward, not a full logical exploration of the subjects at hand. And that, by definition, is what creates the feeling of melodrama as opposed to true drama.

To avoid this, writers often remove the counterpoint to the Crucial Element from the archetype who is opposite to the Main Character and give that one element to some other archetype. This effectively moves the Obstacle Character point of view from the opposite archetype to the new one. In this manner, the Main Character now has two separate relationships – a plot based one with its archetype opposite and the human quality argument with the archetype who is the new Obstacle Character. In essence the single relationship that held both arguments is now split into two relationships creating the classic "Dramatic Triangle".

In this more refined arrangement, the Main Character and its associate archetype have it out with its opposite archetype in the plot and the Main Character point of view comes into conflict with the other archetype who now has added that opposite of the Crucial Element. That other character is often the "Love Interest" or some other personally connected character who argues with the Main Character about the proper way to comport itself, even as the Main Character is battling its archetypal opposite over the goal.

How to Create Archetypal Characters

Just because characters are Archetypal does not mean they cannot be fresh and interesting. Archetypal Characters have just as many diverse characteristics as Complex Characters. The only difference is how these characteristics are divided among your story's characters. When an equal number are given to each character and when all the elements making up each character are from a single "family" of elements, Archetypal Characters are created. In this sense, an Archetypal Character set is like an alignment of the planets: each individual orbit is complex, but we choose to observe them when they are all lined up in a clear and simple pattern.

Nonetheless, we must still explore all aspects of each character to make the Story Mind's argument fully. However, since there is such consistency to the way the elements are distributed, the audience will anticipate the content of each character, allowing an author the luxury of using shortcuts to describe them. In fact, once a character is outlined enough to establish its Archetypal tendency, an author can leave out the rest of the information since the audience will fill it in anyway. In a sense, a character is guilty of being Archetypal until proven otherwise.

A Sample Story Using Archetypes

When an author wishes to concentrate primarily on action or entertainment, it is often best to take advantage of the Archetypal arrangement to fully make the story's argument with a minimum of exposition. The characters still need to be interesting in order to involve an audience in their story. To illustrate how even Archetypal characters can be intriguing, let's create story using only Archetypes and dress them up in some attractive storytelling.

Creating a Protagonist

We want to write a simple story using Archetypal Characters. We can create a PROTAGONIST called Jane. Jane wants to... what?... rob a bank?...kill the monster?... stop the terrorists?... resolve her differences with her mother? It really doesn't matter; her goal can be whatever interests us as authors. So we'll pick "stop the terrorists" because it interests us. All right, our Protagonist —

Jane — wants to stop the terrorists.

Creating an Antagonist

Dramatica says we need an ANTAGONIST. Antagonist by definition is the person who tries to prevent achievement of the goal. So, who might be diametrically against the completion of the task Jane wants to accomplish? The Religious Leader whose dogma is the source of inspiration that spawns the acts of terror?... The multinational business cartel that stands to make billions if the terrorists succeed in their scheme?... Her former lover who leads the elite band of criminals? We like THAT one! Okay, we have our Protagonist (Jane) who wants to stop the terrorists who are led by her former lover (Johann).

Creating a Skeptic

Two simple Characters down, six to go. Dramatica now tells us we need a SKEPTIC. Who might oppose the effort and disbelieve in the ultimate success of good Jane? A rival special agent who doesn't want to be left in the dust by her glowing success?... Her current love interest on the force who feels Jane is in over her head?... Her father, the Senator, who wants his daughter to follow him into politics? Good enough for us. So we have Jane who wants to stop the terrorists, pitted against her former lover Johann who heads the criminal band, and opposed by her father, the Senator.

Creating a Sidekick

To balance the Skeptic, we're going to need a SIDEKICK. We could bring back her current lover but *this* time have him knowing how much ridding the world of scum-sucking pigs appeals to Jane so he remains steadfastly behind her. Or we might employ her Supervisor and mentor on the force who knows the depth of Jane's talent, wants to inspire other young idealists to take action against threats to democracy, or prove his theories and vindicate his name in the undercover world… We'll use the Supervisor. So here's Jane who wants to stop the terrorists, pitted against her former lover Johann, the head of the band who wants to stop her, opposed by her father, the Senator, and supported by her Supervisor.

Creating a Contagonist

Let's bring in a CONTAGONIST: the Seasoned Cop who says, "You have to play by the rules" and thwarts Jane's efforts to forge a better modus operandi?… Or, the Ex-Con with a heart of gold who studies the classics and counsels her to base her approach on proven scenarios?… Or, her friend Sheila, a computer whiz who has a bogus response plan based on averaging every scenario every attempted? Computer whiz it is. So Jane wants to stop the terrorists, is pitted against the head of the band (her former lover Johann) who wants to stop her, opposed by her father, the Senator, supported by her Supervisor, and tempted by her friend Sheila, the computer whiz.

Creating a Guardian

Keeping in mind the concept of Dynamic Pairs, we are going to want to balance the Computer Whiz with a GUARDIAN. The Master of the Oriental martial arts who urges her to "go with the flow" ("Use The Force, Jane!")?… The Ex-Con again who urges, "Get back to basics"?… or perhaps the Seasoned Cop who paves the way through the undercover jungle?…. We like the Seasoned Cop. Note how we could have used him as Contagonist, but elected to use him as Guardian instead. It's totally up to us as authors as to which characteristics go into which players. Jane wants to stop the terrorists, is pitted against the head of the band (her former lover Johann) who wants to stop her, is opposed by her father, the Senator, supported by her Supervisor, tempted by her friend Sheila the computer whiz, and protected by the Seasoned Cop.

38

Creating Reason and Emotion Characters

Since we really like some of our earlier concepts for Characters, let's use the Ex-Con as REASON, stressing the need to use classic scenarios. We'll balance her with the Master of the Oriental martial arts, who maintains Jane's need to break with the Western approach by letting loose and following her feelings. Well, that seems to cover all eight Archetypal Characters: Protagonist, Antagonist, Skeptic, Sidekick, Contagonist, Guardian, Reason and Emotion. Finally, we have Jane who wants to stop the terrorists and is pitted against the head of the band (her former lover Johann) who wants to stop her, is opposed by her Father, the Senator, is supported by her Supervisor, tempted by her friend Sheila the computer whiz, protected by the Seasoned Cop, urged by the Ex-Con to copy the classics, and counseled by the Master of Oriental martial arts to let loose and follow her feelings.

Character Archetypes in Dynamic Pairs

Dynamic Pairs

We have now created four distinct pairs of Archetypal Characters. Each pair presents the birthing ground of a particular kind of conflict. Two Characters bonded in such a relationship constitute a *Dynamic Pair.* Here are the Eight Archetypal Characters organized by Dynamic Pairs.

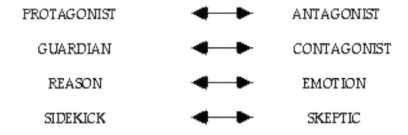

Functions of Dynamic Pairs

We can easily see how these Archetypal pairs represent a broad analogy to a human mind dealing with a problem. The Protagonist represents the desire to work at resolving a problem. Its Dynamic Pair, the Antagonist represents the reticence to change things. As with the Archetypal Characters, we all face an internal battle between making decisions based upon Reason or upon Emotion. Like the functions of the Sidekick and Skeptic, the Story Mind will engage in a struggle between Faith and Disbelief. And finally in an Archetypal sense, the Mind will be torn between the Contagonist's temptation for immediate gratification and the Guardian's counsel to consider the consequences.

Matching Character Personalities to Archetypes

There is much to be gained by populating a story with interesting personalities, but personalities are not necessarily functioning characters. You can have as many "window dressing" characters as you want. Make sure, however, that each of the **eight archetypes** is represented by one of your characters.

For a given character, why would you pick one archetypal function over another? Simple: the archetypal functions are the foundations of different personality types. Take the Sidekick archetype, for example. The Sidekick is described as a "faithful supporter." If you select a character as the Sidekick, you have already said a lot about the kind of person it will be.

Note that the archetypal description says nothing about in what the character has faith or what it supports. This is why Toto in The Wizard of Oz can be a sidekick, but so can Renfield in Dracula. The Sidekick is not necessarily the faithful supporter of the Protagonist, but simply fulfills the dramatic function of illustrating

40

how the qualities of faith and support fare in regard to solving the story's central problem.

So, in choosing which archetypes you want to assign to which characters, select the matches in which the characters function best reflects its personality, and vice versa.

Archetypes Have Their Place, But....

Archetypal Characters have their place, mind you. If an author's focus is on Plot or Theme, he may want to create easily identifiable Archetypes as a kind of shorthand to save space and time.

As soon as the edges of an Archetypal Character are sketched out, audiences (who have seen these Archetypes time and again) will fill in the rest, pending information to the contrary. In this way, an author can free up time or pages for aspects of the story that may be much more interesting to him.

As a result, Complex Characters are often the first things torn down in an effort to conserve media real estate. This leads to a glut of action-oriented stories populated by stick-figure people. Whenever there is a glut in one place, you will find a deficiency somewhere else. The imbalance between glut and deficiency creates demand. Box office is directly proportional to demand. No more need be said.

Methodology Archetypes

Before the final version of *Dramatica – a New Theory of Story* there was an earlier draft that contained unfinished concepts and additional theory ultimately deemed "too complex". As a result, this material was never fully developed, was cut from the final version of the book, and has never seen the light of day — until now! Recently, a copy of this early draft surfaced in the theory archives. The following are excerpts from this "lost" text.

CAVEAT:

Because the text that follows was not fully developed, portions may be incomplete, inaccurate, or actually quite wrong.

It is presented as a look into the history of the development of Dramatica and also as a source of additional theory concepts that (with further development) may prove useful.

Introduction

This segment represents a whole new, previously unmentioned aspect of Archetypal Characters. After developing the original eight Archetypes and their Elements with Chris, based on character motivations, I went on to consider what the Archetypes might look like in terms of their Methodologies, Evaluations, and Purposes.

Theory-wise, if the Problem Element of the Objective Story falls in one of these other dimensions of characters, then the Elements in those dimensions would be the principal ones by which the Archetypes would be known. In effect, the set of 16 Elements which contains the Problem Element creates its own, unique "flavor" or variety of Archetypes.

Often, the original 8 Archetypes can seem limiting and lead authors into creating complex characters when, in fact, all that is really needed is another flavor of Archetypes.

This excerpt describes the first 8 of 24 new Archetypes.

Methodology Archetypes

When we began our exploration of Characters, we divided them into eight Simple Archetypes, based on their Motivations. Similarly, as we begin our exploration of Method, we discover eight Simple Methodologies that the Simple Characters employ. As before, we divide them into two quads: one reflecting Action Methodologies and the other, Decision Methodologies.

The Action Methodology Archetypes are Assertive, Passive, Responsive, and Preservative. Let's take a look at each.

ASSERTIVE: The Assertive approach is based on the "first strike" concept. When one's method is Assertive, she will take the initiative action to achieve her goal or obtain what she wants. .

RESPONSIVE: In Contrast, the Responsive will act only when provoked, but will then retaliate, seeking to eliminate the threat to her status quo.

PRESERVATIVE: The Preservative methodology is to build back what has been diminished and take steps to guard things against further encroachment. Unlike the Responsive Methodology, the Preservative approach will not strike back against the source of the encroachment but shield against it.

PASSIVE: The Passive approach will be to "go with the flow" and hope things get better by themselves, rather than attempting to improve them.

It is important to note that Assertive and Passive are not the Dynamic pair in this group. Rather, Assertive and Responsive complement each other. This can be seen by thinking in terms of the borders of a country. Assertive and Responsive will both cross the border, one for a first strike, the other only in retaliation. But Passive and Preservative will **never** cross the border, one allowing itself to be overrun, and one building defenses.

Whereas the Action Methodologies indicate the approach to manipulation of the environment that is acceptable to a given Character, the Decision Methodologies indicate the mental approach that will be acceptable. The Decision Methodologies are Dogmatic, Pragmatic, Cautious, and Risky.

DOGMATIC: The Dogmatic approach will only consider data that has been "proven" as being correct. Speculative or second-hand information is rejected out of hand.

PRAGMATIC: In opposition to that approach the Pragmatic Methodology widens their considerations to include information that may prove to be correct based on circumstantial evidence.

CAUTIOUS: When one decides in a Cautious manner, she determines the relative likelihood of various data, giving greater weight in her considerations to information that appears more certain.

RISKY: The Risky approach considers all information that is not definitely ruled out as incorrect, giving all data equal weight in the Decision process regardless of its likelihood.

In the Decision Methodologies, Dogmatic pairs with Pragmatic, and Cautious complements Risky. As a group these four Action and four Decision approaches constitute the Eight Simple Methodologies, and make up our first organization of Plot. We know these types, don't we? They appear in our world, they appear in our stories, they appear in ourselves. They appear in our stories *because* they appear in ourselves. As with the Eight Simple Characters, they can be divided in Quads.

The Eight Simple Methodologies

The Action Quad

RESPONSIVE

PASSIVE

PRESERVATIVE

ASSERTIVE

The Decision Quad

PRAGMATIC

RISKY

CAUTIOUS

DOGMATIC

As with the Eight Simple Characters: **No Character should represent more than one Methodology in a given Dynamic Pair**. In other words, just as one Character should not be the Protagonist *and* Antagonist, one Character should not be Assertive *and* Responsive.

Now you may have noticed that every time we talk about the Methodologies we speak of them as the ways in which Characters act or decide. The immediate question that comes to mind is whether or not these Simple Methodologies of Plot are tied to specific Simple Characters. Let's find out.

Archetypal Methodologies in Star Wars

Returning to Star Wars, we can analyze the Method each Simple Character employs to see if: a) they limit themselves to one, and b) if there is a match between Character *Motivation* and Character *Method*.

Certainly Obi Wan seems RESPONSIVE. He never attacks, just responds to attacks , such as the Cantina scene where he cuts off the creature's arm *after* it had attacked Luke. But here the direct relationship to the motivation archetype pattern breaks down.

This time Obi is not balanced by Darth but by the Empire, which is the key ASSERTIVE Character in the story. This is exemplified in the Empire's unprovoked attack on Leia's home world of Alderan, and their efforts to track down and destroy the rebel base. Darth takes on a PRESERVATIVE approach, which works nicely with his charge to recover the stolen plans. Every step he takes is an attempt to get back to start. Even when he leads his fighters into the trench on the Death Star, he cautions his henchmen not to chase those who break off from the attack, but to stay on the leader.

Rounding out the Four Simple Action Methodologies, Luke fills the role of PASSIVE. Luke, Passive? Yep. When Uncle Owen tells Luke that he must stay on one more season, Luke argues, but does he accept it? When Obi tells Luke that he must go with him to Alderan, where does he end up? When the Cantina Bartender tells him the droids must stay outside, does he even argue?

Looking at the Decision Quad, Han reads very well as the DOGMATIC approach, which matches nicely with his role as Skeptic. Leia, on the other hand is clearly Pragmatic, adapting to new and unexpected situations as needed. Note the way Dogmatic Han screws up the rescue attempt in the detention block with his inability to adapt, compared to Leia blasting a hole in the corridor wall, manufacturing an escape route.

Interestingly, the joint Sidekick of R2D2 and C3PO is split by the Methodologies of RISKY and CAUTIOUS. R2D2 is always the one jumping into the fray, going out on a limb, trailblazing through blaster fire. In Contrast, C3PO doesn't want to go into the escape pod, doesn't want to go on R2's "mission" to find Obi, and excels at hiding from battle whenever he gets the chance.

If we hang the Star Wars Character names on the Simple Methodology QUAD we get:

Action Quad

RESPONSIVE – OBI WAN

PASSIVE – LUKE   *PRESERVATIVE* – DARTH

ASSERTIVE - EMPIRE

Decision Quad

PRAGMATIC – LEIA PRAGMATIC

RISKY – R2D2

CAUTIOUS – C3PO

DOGMATIC – HAN

For the first time we begin to get a sense of some of the conflicts between Characters that we *felt* in Star Wars, but were not explained by the Motivations of the Simple Characters alone. For example, we can see that in terms of Methodology, Obi is now in direct conflict with the Empire. Suddenly the scene where he is stopped along with Luke by the Storm Troopers on the way into

Mos Eisley makes much more sense, as does the scene where he must avoid the Storm Troopers and deactivate the Tractor Beam.

From the Methodology standpoint, Luke is now diametrically opposed to Darth, and that defines that additional conflict between them that does not grow from Luke as Protagonist and Darth as Contagonist. The scene in the Trench where Darth attacks Assertively and Luke ignores him with calm Passivity is a fine example of this.

The antagonism (appropriate word) between Leia and Han has a firm grounding in the Dogmatic versus Pragmatic approach. This is what gives that extra edge between them that is not created by their Simple Characters of Reason and Skeptic.

Of particular note is how R2D2 and C3PO, who share a Character role of Sidekick, are split into a conflicting Dynamic Pair of Risky and Cautious. So many of their scenes have them diverging, even while loyally following Luke. The sniping that goes on between them is a direct result of their opposing Methodologies, and enriches what otherwise would be a flat relationship. After all, if they both agreed with each other's approach AND were jointly the Sidekick as well, how could you even tell them apart, other than by the shape of their costumes?

Finally, notice how poor Chewbacca ended up with no Methodology at all. Perhaps that explains why he never really *does* anything.

From the chart we can see that the opposition of Dynamic Pairs between Characters is not necessarily carried over into their Methodologies. Indeed, some Characters might be in conflict over principles but not in approach, and vice versa. This relationship between the Motivation Level and the Methodology Level is the embryonic beginning of more believable "3 dimensional" or "well rounded" Characters. To get a more clear understanding of this phenomenon, we can put the Simple Character Quads side by side with the Simple Methodology Quad.

Driver Motivation Quad   **Action Methodology Quad**

LUKE PROTAGONIST		**LUKE** PASSIVE	
OBI WAN GUARDIAN	**DARTH** CONTAGONIST	**OBI WAN** RESPONSIVE	**EMPIRE** ASSERTIVE
EMPIRE ANTAGONIST		**DARTH** PRESERVATIVE	

Passenger Motivation Quad   **Decision Methodology Quad**

R2D2 + C3PO SIDEKICK		**LEIA** PRAGMATIC	
CHEWBACA EMOTION			
	LEIA REASON	**R2D2** RISKY	**C3PO** CAUTIOUS
HAN SKEPTIC		**HAN** DOGMATIC	

When viewed in this manner, the ebb and flow of conflict can be seen as not a single relationship between Characters, but a complex multi-level interrelationship. Yet, we are still dealing here with *Simple* Methodologies. Just as we had found that each of the Eight Simple Characters contained two components, the Eight Simple Methodologies are composed of two aspects as well: Attitude and Approach. As before, let's separate the Simple Methodologies into their respective components.

The Sixteen Methodologies

ASSERTIVE

Approach Plogistic (*plot logistic)*:

The assertive character takes **Proaction** to upset a stable environment in order to achieve her goals.

Attitude Plogistic:

She **Evaluates** her situation to determine what action she should take.

RESPONSIVE

Approach Plogistic:

When Responsive, a character **Reacts** to changes in her environment.

Attitude Plogistic:

The Responsive **Re-evaluates** her environment in light of unwanted changes, and creates a goal to recapture stability.

PRESERVATIVE

Approach Plogistic:

This character employs **Protection** to prevent what she has from being eroded.

Attitude Plogistic:

She is driven by **Non-Acceptance**of the diminishing of her situation.

PASSIVE

Approach Plogistic:

The Passive character exists in **Inaction**, making no move to counter threats against her.

Attitude Plogistic:

She**Accepts** whatever comes her way. Attitude Plogistic: She **Accepts** whatever comes her way.

DOGMATIC

Approach Plogistic:

Dogmatic deals only in **Actualities**. Approach Plogistic: Dogmatic deals only in **Actualities**.

Attitude Plogistic:

She relies on **Deduction** to reduce data to an irrefutable conclusion.

PRAGMATIC

Approach Plogistic:

The Pragmatic concerns herself with **Potentialities**, looking at all alternative explanations that can be created from existing data.

Attitude Plogistic:

She employs **Induction** to generate alternatives.

CAUTIOUS

Approach Plogistic:

The Cautious character bases her decisions on **Probabilities**: the most likely of alternatives.

Attitude Plotgistic:

She uses **Reduction** to narrow the field of conceivable alternatives.

RISKY

Approach Plogistic:

The Risky character considers all **Possibilities** equally, regardless of their relative likelihood.

Attitude Plogistic:

She processes information with **Production** to create any alternatives that are *not ruled out* by known data.

Placing these Plogistics in a Quad table we get:

Internal Approach		External Approach	
	ACTUALITY		PROACTION
PROBABILITY	POSSIBILITY	PROTECTION	INACTION
	POTENTIALITY		RE-ACTION

Internal Attitude		External Attitude	
	DEDUCTION		EVALUATION
REDUCTION	PRODUCTION	NON-ACCEPTANCE	ACCEPTANCE
	INDUCTION		RE-EVALUATION

Looking at these sixteen Methodologies, it is important to remember what they represent. DRAMATICA looks at each and every element of story structure as an aspect of the Story Mind dealing with a problem. And we can clearly see that these sixteen points represent part of that process.

When examining our environment, we all make Evaluations, Re-Evaluate in light of a changing situation, choose whether to Accept our lot or Not Accept it. We all employ Deduction to determine what we know, Induction to keep our minds open to other explanations, Reduction to determine what is most likely, and Production to be creative. From these we establish what we see as Actuality, Potentiality, Probability, and Possibility, as well as the need for Proaction, Reaction, Protection, or Inaction.

Once again, in stories, these Methodologies can be illustrated in individual Characters or combined in ways that do not violate their potential. The Dramatica rules for combining characteristics apply here as well.

Based upon these rules, we can easily create our own multi-level Characters. Let's return to the simple story we wrote about Joan, the Screenplay writer.

As you'll recall, we created Joan, the Protagonist, who wants to write a screenplay. She was in conflict with the Studio Executive, our Antagonist, who wanted to sell a screenplay of her own instead. Joan's father was a Skeptic, not believing in his daughter's talent, but Joan's writing teacher was her faithful Sidekick. As Contagonist, we created Joan's friend, the Computer Whiz, who tempts Joan to use "the System". Guardian to Joan is the Seasoned Writer, who keeps the execs of her tail and counsels her to be true to herself. The Prostitute, a student of the Classics served as Reason, and the Avant Guard Artist was Emotion.

As an exercise, let's assign each of these Eight Simple Characters one of the Eight Simple Methodologies. As we've already determined, there is no requirement that a particular Methodology must be matched to a particular Character. So, if we start with Joan who is of primary importance to us, which one of the Methodologies do we like best for our Protagonist? We have a choice of Assertive, Reactive, Preservative, Passive, Dogmatic, Pragmatic, Cautious, and Risky.

Try each one against what we know of Joan. It is clear that any of the eight would create a believable and much more three dimensional Character than the simple Protagonist by herself. And yet, there will be some combinations that will appeal to one

54

Author that are not at all acceptable to another. Protagonist Joan as an Assertive young writer, or Protagonist Joan as Risk taker? Our hero, the adamant, close-minded Dogmatist, or the Passive putz? Is she to be Reactive to every ripple in her pond, or Cautious about every move she makes. Doe she try to Preserve what she already has, or take a Pragmatic approach, adapting to a changing scenario? The choices are all valid, and all open to you, the Author.

For our tastes (where they happen to be after lunch as we write this) let's pick a Risky Protagonist. So Joan, the "wanna-be" Script Writer is a real Risk taker, jumping across the stream and looking for the next stone while in mid air. So what kinds of things will this reckless writer do? She'll wager her contract on being able to make a waitress cry with the sentence she scrawled on a napkin in the diner. If her mother's health is failing because she can only afford half the dosage of essential medication that she needs, she'll spend the medication money to fix her broken typewriter so she can finish her outline and get enough of an advance (if they like it) to buy her the full dose. Real Risk taker, our Joan!

So now, we have the rival Studio Exec, our Antagonist. And she can be any one of the seven remaining Methodologies. We could put her in direct conflict of Methodologies as well as Characteristics, by making her the Cautious type. As such, she would lay out all the ground work to assure that her script will be chosen, leaving nothing to chance. Or she could be Responsive, and attack Joan every time she sees Joan's advancement as threatening her own. Or she could be Assertive and attack Joan without provocation, because she feels it will help her own cause. We'll pick Assertive, because we want an Action story, and our Protagonist is not an action Character.

We continue in this manner until we have assigned a Simple Methodology to each Simple Character. So, finally, we have Risky Joan, who wants to write a screenplay and is embattled against the Assertive studio Executive who wants to stop her, opposed by her Preservationist Father, supported by her Passive Teacher, tempted by her friend, the Cautious Computer Whiz, protected by the Responsive Seasoned Writer, counseled by the Dogmatic Prostitute to copy the classics, and urged by the Pragmatic Avant Guard Artist to break new ground.

This is beginning to sound a lot less like other stories we've seen before. And that is just with the Simple Motivations and Methodologies. When you figure in complex Motivations and Methodologies by mixing and matching sixteen Motivations with sixteen Methodologies, then group them together in uneven ways: more to some Characters and fewer to others, you can begin to see the great variety of Characters that can be created using the DRAMATICA structure. And that is the real beauty of DRAMATICA. Because it is a system of interrelationships, a relatively small number of variables creates an astronomical number of specific structures. Form without Formula. And it works because it mirrors the structure and functioning of our own minds in the Story Mind.

Continuing along that parallel, we can see that the Story Mind in dealing with a problem will not only be motivated and apply a methodology, but will also monitor feedback to determine the effectiveness of the method and the propriety of the motivation. This function is defined by our third level of Character, Evaluation.

Evaluation Archetypes

Before the final version of *Dramatica – a New Theory of Story* there was an earlier draft that contained unfinished concepts and additional theory ultimately deemed "too complex". As a result, this material was never fully developed, was cut from the final version of the book, and has never seen the light of day — until now! Recently, a copy of this early draft surfaced in the theory archives. The following are excerpts from this "lost" text.

CAVEAT:

Because the text that follows was not fully developed, portions may be incomplete, inaccurate, or actually quite wrong.

It is presented as a look into the history of the development of Dramatica and also as a source of additional theory concepts that (with further development) may prove useful.

Introduction

This segment represents a whole new, previously unmentioned aspect of Archetypal Characters. After developing the original eight Archetypes and their Elements with Chris, I went on to consider what the Archetypes might look like in the Methodologies, Evaluations, and Purposes. Theory-wise, if the Problem Element of the Objective Story falls in one of these other dimensions of characters, then the Elements in those dimensions would be the principal ones by which the Archetypes would be known. In effect, the set of 16 Elements which contains the Problem Element creates its own, unique "flavor" or variety of Archetypes.

Often, the original 8 Archetypes can seem limiting and lead authors into creating complex characters when, in fact, all that is really needed is another flavor of Archetypes.

This excerpt describes the second group of 8 of 24 new Archetypes.

Means of Evaluation

As there were Eight Simple Motivation Characters and Eight Simple Methodology Character, we might expect there to be Eight Simple Evaluation Characters, and so there are. A Character might evaluate using Calculation, or Guesswork. She could base her evaluation on Information or Intuition. She might consider the Outcome of an effort or the Means employed to achieve that Outcome. Finally, she might expand her considerations to include the Intent behind the effort and the actual Impact that effort has had.

Putting these Eight Simple Evaluations in Quad form we get:

The Eight Simple Evaluations

The Measuring Quad

INFORMATION

CALCULATION   INTUITION

GUESSWORK

OUTCOME

MEANS   IMPACT

INTENT

We can see the patterns of dynamic pairs created between the Eight Simple Evaluations. Let's define each term for a more complete understanding of their relationships.

Calculation: The Calculating Character establishes an unbroken chain of relationships that leads to a conclusion. Her thinking will only carry her as far as the chain can be extended. As soon as she cannot make one thing lead *directly* to the next, she will not entertain any speculations beyond that point.

Intuition: The Intuitive Character forms her conclusions from circumstantial or nebulous input, rather than a definitive line of logic.

Information: The Character who relies on Information will entertain in her deliberations only definitive packets of data.

Guesswork: The Character who Guesses will fill in the blanks in her information with what appears most likely to go there.

Outcome: The Outcome measuring Character is only concerned with the immediate nature of the objective: whether or not, or how well it has been met.

Impact: Measuring Impact, a Character looks at the ripples in the big picture created by a particular outcome, or looks how well an objective accomplished that for which it was intended.

Means: The Character measuring Means in most concerned with *how* an Objective was met rather than if it was or how well.

Intent: When a Character measures Intent, she is concerned with the expectations behind the effort that led to the Outcome, whether or not the Outcome was achieved.

Again, these are aspects of Character we have seen before and are familiar with. In our case, their existence and definitions came as no surprise. Rather, we had just never previously considered them all at once as a group in which we could clearly see the relationships among them.

The real value to us as Authors comes in being able to mix and match Motivations, Methodologies and Evaluations. For example, should we be at work building a Character whose nature is best described as Guardian, we might select Dogmatic as her method and Calculation as her tool of evaluation. So this fellow might protect the Protagonist while stubbornly maintaining an ideology, but evaluating the progress of the quest in a very calculated manner: a Character of some individuality and depth.

What if we had the same Dogmatic Guardian who employed Guesswork instead. We can feel the difference in her nature as a result of this change. Now she would protect the Protagonist, stubbornly maintain an ideology, but base her evaluations of progress on conjecture rather than denotative relationships. Certainly, this person has a wholly different "feel" to her, without being *wholly* different.

The functionality of this is that the way we feel about a Character is based on the sum total of the combined effect of all levels of her attributes. However, when looking at these attributes as separate aspects, we can define the differences between Characters in a precise and specific way in terms of their content and determine if they are nearly the same or completely different. But when we see the dynamic view of the way in which a particular set of aspects merge to create the specific force of a given Character, even a slight change in only one aspect will create a substantially different "feel" to that Character.

When a Character oriented Author writes by "feel" she is sensing the overall impact of a Character's presence. This is not very definable, and therefore dramatic potentials between Characters are often diminished by incomplete understanding of which levels are in conflict between two given Characters, and which are not.

We have already seen an example of this in our analysis of Star Wars. Han (as Skeptic) is only peripherally in conflict with Leia (as Reason). But Han as Dogmatic in directly in conflict with Leia as Pragmatic. If Han and Leia were to argue, there would be much more dramatic potential if they argued over trying a new approach than if they argued over whether or not they ought to take action.

Clearly, the ability to discern the specific nature of the attributes that make up a Character at all levels allows us to precisely define the nature of inter-Character conflicts, without losing sight of the overall feeling that each Character carries with her.

Evaluations in Star Wars

Looking at the Characters of Star Wars in terms of Evaluation only, the arrangement of attributes is a bit murkier. Since this is primarily a story of action, techniques of evaluation do not play a big role in the progress of the story and therefore have been more loosely drawn. Nevertheless, they *are* present, even if there is somewhat less consistency than at the Character or Method levels.

Assigning the Eight Simple Evaluations to the Eight Simple Characters of Star Wars by their most common usage in the story, we generate the following list:

LUKE INFORMATION

EMPIRE CALCULATION

OBI GUESSWORK

DARTH INTUITION

HAN OUTCOME

LEIA INTENT

CHEWY MEANS

C3PO IMPACT

R2D2 ————

Attaching the Character names to the Evaluation Quads we get:

The Eight Simple Evaluations

The Measuring Quad

Luke
INFORMATION

Empire
CALCULATION

Darth
INTUITION

Obi
GUESSWORK

The Measured Quad

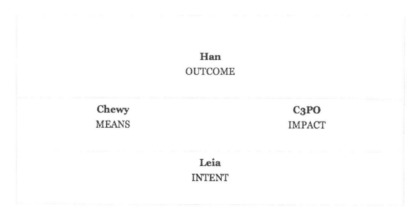

Han
OUTCOME

Chewy
MEANS

C3PO
IMPACT

Leia
INTENT

Again, we can see subtle conflicts in techniques of Evaluation between Characters that are compatible at other levels. For the first time, we can see the tension that as an audience we feel between Darth and the Empire in the "Board Room" scene on the Death Star where Darth constricts the breathing of the general he is "bickering" with. The general says to Darth, "...your sorcerer ways have not helped you conjure up the missing plans...",

63

essentially arguing against Intuition.

Looking at Luke, we note that in his dinner table discussion with Uncle Owen he argues his point that he should be allowed to leave with Information: the new droids are working out, all his friends are at the academy, etc. Another example is the moment Luke bursts into Leia's cell to release her. Rather than use any other technique, he describes the situation to her simply by imparting information: "I'm Luke Skywalker. I'm here to rescue you. I'm here with Ben Kenobi."

Obi Wan, on the other hand, relies on Guesswork when the Millennium Falcon is chasing the lone imperial fighter after coming out of hyperspace. He sees the supposed moon, and guesses, "It's a space station!"

Han is completely Outcome oriented, "I'm just in this for the reward, sister!", and is thereby again in conflict with Leia as Intent: "If money is all you care about, then that's what you'll receive."

Chewy can be seen to focus on Means, when he refuses to don the binders for Luke's plan to rescue Leia.

C3PO is always evaluating impact: " We'll be sent to the spice mines of Kessel", and, "I suggest a different strategy R2... Let the Wookie win."

R2, as noted, does not represent a manner of evaluation. We can see by the feel of his Character that he is motivated and has a method, but he never evaluates anything for himself, you just point him and he goes.

Once again, since Star Wars is an action oriented story, the techniques of Evaluation were not as developed as Motivation and Method.

Sixteen Evaluations

As with the previous two levels of Character, the Eight Simple Evaluations can be divided into sixteen evaluations. In Motivation we had Action and Decision aspects, in Method we had Attitude and Approach. In Evaluation we have Passive and Active.

Calculation:

Passive:

The Calculating Character sees data as Expectations wherein an unbroken chain of relationships that leads to a conclusion.

Active:

To form an Expectation, Calculation develops Theories.

Intuition:

Passive:

The Intuitive Character sees the pattern of her observations in the form of a Determination.

Active:

To arrive at a Determination, Intuitive makes Hunches.

Information:

Passive:

The Character who revolves around Information will entertain in her deliberations only definitive packets of data she sees as

Proven.

Active:

For something to be Proven, the Information Character will institute a Test.

Guesswork:

Passive:

Guesswork will consider even data that is, as of yet, Unproven.

Active:

The system she uses that allows her to accept Unproven data is to Trust.

Outcome:

Passive:

The Outcome measuring Character observes the Results of an effort.

Active:

To see the Results, she looks toward the Ending of the Effort.

Impact:

Passive:

Measuring Impact, a Character looks at the actual Effects of an effort, as opposed to how well it met its charter.

Active:

To determine the Effect, the Impact Character examines how Accurately the ramifications of the effort confine themselves to the targeted goal.

Means:

Passive:

Means is determined by looking at the Process employed in an effort.

Active:

Just as Impact examined Effects in terms of Accuracy, Means examines Process in terms of the Unending aspects of its nature. In essence, Effects are measured by how much they spill over the intended goal, and Process is evaluated by how much of it continues past the intended point of conclusion.

Intent:

Passive:

When a Character measures Intent, she is concerned with the Cause behind the effort.

Active:

She looks at the aspects of the Cause that do Not Accurately reflect the scope of the goal.

Let's look at these sixteen evaluation techniques in Quad form.

Measured Active Set	Measured Passive Set
PROVEN	EFFECT
NON-ACCURATE ACCURATE	PROCESS RESULT
UNPROVEN	CAUSE

Measuring Passive Set	Measuring Active Set
EXPECTATION	THEORY
UNENDING ENDING	TRUST TEST
DETERMINATION	HUNCH

As before, these four groupings constitute the dynamic Quads of the Evaluation Set, and are subject to the same DRAMATICA rules as the characteristic and method sets.

Since all good things come in Quads, and since we have so far explored three sets of Character traits, we might expect a final set to round out that Quad as well. DRAMATICA calls that final set of characteristics, Purposes.

Purpose Archetypes

Purpose Archetypes

Before the final version of *Dramatica – a New Theory of Story* there was an earlier draft that contained unfinished concepts and additional theory ultimately deemed "too complex". As a result, this material was never fully developed, was cut from the final version of the book, and has never seen the light of day — until now! Recently, a copy of this early draft surfaced in the theory archives. The following are excerpts from this "lost" text.

CAVEAT:

Because the text that follows was not fully developed, portions may be incomplete, inaccurate, or actually quite wrong.

It is presented as a look into the history of the development of Dramatica and also as a source of additional theory concepts that (with further development) may prove useful.

Introduction

This segment represents a whole new, previously unmentioned aspect of Archetypal Characters. After developing the original eight Archetypes and their Elements with Chris, I went on to consider what the Archetypes might look like in the Methodologies, Evaluations, and Purposes. Theory-wise, if the Problem Element of the Objective Story falls in one of these other dimensions of characters, then the Elements in those dimensions would be the principal ones by which the Archetypes would be known. In effect, the set of 16 Elements which contains the

Problem Element creates its own, unique "flavor" or variety of Archetypes.

Often, the original 8 Archetypes can seem limiting and lead authors into creating complex characters when, in fact, all that is really needed is another flavor of Archetypes.

This excerpt describes the third and final group of 8 of 24 new Archetypes.

Purpose Archetypes

When a Character of a certain Motivation acts with a particular Method using a specific mode of Evaluation, her directions is dictated by her Purpose. Conversely, Motivation, Method, and Evaluation are directionless without Purpose. As a corollary to that, each of the four aspects of Character requires the other three, and is determined by the other three.

This is our first glimpse of the real interdependencies of Dramatica: that any three elements of a Quad determine the fourth. This is WHY Dramatica works; that the elements of story are not independent, but *inter*dependent.

This being the case, let us list our Eight Simple Motivations along side the Simple Methodologies and the Simple Evaluations, and see if we can predict what the Eight Simple Purposes might be.

Motivations	Methodologies	Evaluations
Protagonist	Assertive	Outcome
Antagonist	Responsive	Impact
Guardian	Dogmatic	Calculation
Contagonist	Pragmatic	Guesswork
Reason	Cautious	Information
Emotion	Risky	Intuition
Sidekick	Passive	Intent
Skeptic	Preservative	Means

When we look at the three points we already have, we can extend that line to project the fourth point, Purpose. When we look at a Protagonist who is Assertive and Evaluates in terms of Outcome, her Purpose is to achieve a Goal. But what then of the Antagonist. The Antagonist, being Responsive and Evaluating Impact, is more concerned with the Requirement.

The Antagonist not Goal-oriented? Absolutely Correct. A TRUE Archetypal Antagonist will be consistent through all four character dimensions. She would be Responsive to the threat of the Protagonist's Assertiveness. She would evaluate in terms of the Impact being felt.

Keep in mind that a villain is not the same as an Antagonist. In fact, stories often cast the villain as the Protagonist so that the story's troubles are a result of the villain's proactive actions. Then, when the hero responds, she is justified. In fact, it is hard to find an Archetypal character who is consistent through all four character dimensions.

Take James Bond, for example. Does he decide that there is something he wants to accomplish and then go after it, starting all the trouble? Not really. Rather, a villain does something to achieve what the villain wants, and Bond Responds.

The point being not to say that James Bond is not a "Protagonist," but simply that he is not a consistent Archetype through all four dimensions.

Purposes of other Archetypes

For clarity, let us describe what the other Archetypes would be like if they followed through to consistent Purposes. Then, we can explore how the attributes might be mixed and matched when building specific characters.

For every Goal, there is a Consequence; for every Requirement, a Cost. The Archetypal Guardian is concerned with the Consequence: it is her Purpose to prevent it. The Contagonist, on the other hand is focused on the Cost: it is her Purpose not to pay it. Note the subtle complexities between the positive Purposes of the Protagonist/Antagonist and the negative Purposes of the Guardian/Contagonist.

So, we have half of our Purposes lined out. Next to the other three levels of Character they look like this:

Motivation	Methodology	Evaluation	Purpose
Protagonist	Assertive	Outcome	Goal
Antagonist	Responsive	Impact	Requirement
Guardian	Dogmatic	Calculation	Consequence
Contagonist	Pragmatic	Guesswork	Cost
Reason	Cautious	Information	
Emotion	Risky	Intuition	
Sidekick	Passive	Intent	
Skeptic	Preservative	Means	

Now, what to do about the Purposes of the remaining four Simple Characters. Harkening back to the terms "Driver" Characters and "Passenger" Characters, we might better describe the Passengers as "Back Seat Drivers". That is to say that just because they are not the prime movers of the *direction* of the story doesn't mean they are not prime movers of *any* part of the story. In fact, they are quite active in determining the *course* of the story.

Just like any journey, a story may focus on the destination, or the sight seeing along the way. Sometimes it is more important where you are going, sometimes how you get there. When a Simple story is destination oriented, the first four Simple Characters are the Drivers. But when a Simple story is journey oriented, the Protagonist, Antagonist, Guardian and Contagonist are relegated to the back seat as Passengers and Reason, Emotion, Sidekick and Skeptic Drive. In fact, all eight are really driving all the time, just in different areas.

What then are these areas? Just as with our minds, the Story Mind's purpose may be one of an External nature or one of and Internal nature. When we want to change our *environment*, we work toward an External Purpose. However, when we want to change *ourselves*, we work toward in Internal Purpose.

Since we have been using Simple action stories in most of our examples, the Externally oriented characters have appeared to be the Drivers. But when we look toward Simple Decision stories, the Internally oriented characters become the Prime Movers.

So what then would be the Internal Purposes that complete the list of Eight Simple Purposes?

Motivation	Methodology	Evaluation	Purpose
Protagonist	Assertive	Outcome	Goal
Antagonist	Responsive	Impact	Requirement
Guardian	Dogmatic	Calculation	Consequence
Contagonist	Pragmatic	Guesswork	Cost
Reason	Cautious	Information	**Satisfaction**
Emotion	Risky	Intuition	**Happiness**
Sidekick	Passive	Intent	**Fulfillment**
Skeptic	Preservative	Means	**Contentment**

 The difference in Purpose between the two groups that make up the Eight Simple Characters is clear. To see how these Purposes fit in with the Motivation, Methodology, and Evaluation traits, lets examine the Internal Characters one by one.

When you look at the Character of Reason, who Cautiously evaluates things in terms of Information, the Purpose of Satisfaction fits right in. To her counterpart, Emotion, doing things in a Risky manner based on Intuition, Happiness is the Purpose to which they aspire. Similarly, the Passive Sidekick evaluating the Intent, rather than the success, is a perfect supporter seeking only Fulfillment. Her adversary, the Skeptic, trying to Preserve her situation, not concerned with whether the Intent is for the good so much as what Means must be employed, finds her Purpose eventual Contentment.

If a Simple story is about trying to achieve a Goal, the Antagonist will be the Prime Mover. If a Simple story is about trying to reach Fulfillment, the Sidekick will be the Prime Mover.

Sixteen Purposes

What remains is to separate the Eight Simple Purposes into the sixteen Purpose traits. Since we have seen that either the External Characters or the Internal Characters can be the Drivers depending upon the type of story, Each of these simple Purposes can be split into a *Situation* Purpose and a *Condition* focus to their Simple Purpose.

Goal:

Situation Focus:

Actuality

Condition Focus:

Awareness

Consequence:

Situation Focus:

Chaos

Condition Focus:

Inequity

Requirement:

Situation Focus:

Ability

Condition Focus:

Knowledge

Cost:

Situation Focus:

Change

Condition Focus:

Speculation

Satisfaction:

Situation Focus:

Projection

Condition Focus:

Inertia

Happiness:

Situation Focus:

Desire

Condition Focus:

Thought

Fulfillment:

Situation Focus:

Self-Awareness

Condition Focus:

Perception

Contentment:

Situation Focus:

Order

Condition Focus:

Equity

Here are the sixteen Conclusions in Quad form:

External Condition Focus		External Situation Focus	
KNOWLEDGE		ABILITY	
AWARE	ACTUALITY	PROJECTION	INERTIA
EQUITY		ORDER	

Internal Situation Focus		Internal Condition Focus	
DESIRE		THOUGHT	
SPECULATION	CHANGE	SELF-AWARE	PERCEPTION
CHAOS		INEQUITY	

Once more we have *an* arrangement of the sixteen elements into Quads, but not necessarily the most *useful* arrangement. As we described before, each of the valid arrangements is most appropriate to Character, Audience, or Author. As Authors we want to put things in the best perspective for *our* understanding. One of the beauties of DRAMATICA is that if something is adjusted from *one* valid perspective, it will be equally functional from *all* other valid perspectives, although not necessarily as meaningful.

This arrangement of the Conclusions is the fully Internal or Character perspective. This is the way we, as individuals, tend to group our Conclusions about ourselves and our environment. We see the elements of the upper left Quad are topped by Knowledge. And to us, these four elements describe what we know about the Universe itself. All of them pertain directly to our understanding of what is out there. In contrast, the upper right Quad deals with our physical *relationship* with the Universe. These are the Conclusions we draw about how we can affect our environment and how it affects us. This Quad is appropriately headed by "Ability".

Shifting gears, we move to two Quads that describe our understanding of our Minds and our *mental* relationship with the Universe. The lower left Quad Concludes how we *feel* about our environment, aptly led by "Desire". The lower right Quad organizes our Conclusions about ourselves, described prominently by "Thought".

But what if we step out of that perspective for the moment and deal with these sixteen elements as if we were looking at someone *else's* Mind. More precisely: looking *into* someone else's Mind. We would see that Knowledge, Ability, Desire, and Thought are Conclusions that are the actual *motivators* for that individual. In truth, the other three elements of each Quad are used to arrive at those four motivating Conclusions. So to from a completely External view – the Author's Perspective – we would group Knowledge, Ability, Desire, and Thought together to form a Quad.

From the External view, Inertia and Change are objective traits of the Universe itself. Equally objective (from the External view) are Actuality and Perception. From the outside perspective, Actuality is the true nature of the Universe, whereas Perception is the true nature of our limited appreciation of it. Since there is always more to see than we have seen, Perception can never match Actuality. But in a limited sense, for a particular consideration, Perception can *approach* Actuality. So, from the External Author's view, another Quad consisting of Inertia, Change, Actuality, and Perception is created.

Awareness and Self-Awareness describe the degree of our understanding of all the substances and forces in play, both in our environment and ourselves. Projection and Speculation, however, push that understanding into the future, which, due to our limited Perceptions, has the possibility of being to some degree inaccurate. Nevertheless, it is the best we can do with what we currently Know. So, from the Author's perspective, Awareness, Self-Awareness, Projection, and Speculation define a third Quad.

The remaining elements, Order, Chaos, Equity, and Inequity can be grouped together to describe a Mind's understanding of the *meaning* of the situation, which includes the meaning of the environment *by itself*, and in reference *to self*. Therefore, our final Author's perspective Quad consists of Order, Chaos, Equity, and Inequity.

With this new arrangement, the Quads appear like this:

External Rating Set   **External Judgement Set**

KNOWLEDGE   ACTUALITY

          ABILITY   CHANGE

DESIRE   INERTIA

          THOUGHT   PERCEPTION

	Internal Judgement Set			Internal Rating Set
	ORDER		AWARE	
	INEQUITY	SPECULATION		
EQUITY				PROJECTION
	CHAOS		SELF-AWARE	

As we examine the Author's Perspective arrangement, we get an entirely different "feel" for how we might use these Quads. In terms of designing Characters as and Author, these are the Dynamic Quads we would not want to violate: for the greatest dramatic potential, we would place no more than one trait from each Dynamic Quad in a single Character. Otherwise, the representation of the individual elements becomes easily muddled and unclear to the Audience.

As before, the DRAMATICA rules apply:

1. "Character" is a consistent combination of motivations, methodologies, evaluations and conclusions.

2. Characters should never represent more than one characteristic, methodology, evaluation, or conclusion from the same Dynamic Pair.

3. A physical "host" may contain up to sixty-four Characters.

4. A physical "host" should contain only one Character at a time.

Each Archetype is an Equation

For all you Dramatica "theory hounds" out there, here's one of the newest parts of the theory that grew out of my ongoing development of the new dynamic model of story structure.

Dramatica theory has always had eight equations that describe the relationships among elements in a quad. They are all based on permutations of the initial equation we discovered, which was $T/K = AD$.

Turns out, the dramatic nature of each of the eight archetypal characters in Dramatica is described by one of the eight equations. Now that's pretty amazing – that characters who represent families of thought within our own minds can be described mathematically.

I'm writing a complete and lengthy article on this right now, but it will take a week or so, and I couldn't wait to share this new insight with the Dramatica Theory Hounds. You guys are such avid and loyal students of the underlying principals of Dramatica that I've decided to let you in on every new insight, even before I have time to properly work out the details and present a solid argument for it.

I'll end by saying the while the eight equations describe the natures of the eight archetypes, they do not describe their functions. For that, eight other equations are needed. And these dynamic equations are at the heart of the dynamic model.

They are the process of justification and can be seen in how the quad of Knowledge, Thought, Ability and Desire evolves through three other quads beginning with Can, Need, Want and Should, on to Situation, Circumstances, Sense of Self and State of Being, and ending in Commitment, Rationalization, Responsibility and Obligation.

I've touched on this process of justification in previous articles, and in fact it was worked out even before we created the Dramatica Table of Story Elements some twenty years ago. But, we moved away from the justification process to focus on the structural elements and then flipped and rotated the structural model to show the effects of justification and how it influenced the relationships among dramatic elements to create a storyform.

But, in truth, it did not describe *why* those forces are at work, and that is the issue at hand in the dynamic model.

All for now, gotta go take a walk in the woods.

Conclusion

Archetypes can be seen simply as families of consideration within our own minds. They can be seen as categories of character elements – basic building blocks of our psychologies that can be combined and assembled in a complex ways. They can be seen the foundations of our personalities and as stereotypes, wrapped in the obscurity of role, position and purpose.

In the end, archetypes are no more than convenient constructs with which to ensure the full compliment of human qualities are represented in a story and no less than avatars for the largest components of our hearts and minds.

Printed in Great Britain
by Amazon